AL-GHAZZALI
ON DISCIPLINING THE SELF

Ḥujjat al-Islām Abū Ḥāmid
Muḥammad Ghazzālī Ṭūsī

TRANSLATED FROM THE PERSIAN BY
MUHAMMAD NUR ABDUS SALAM

INTRODUCTION BY
LALEH BAKHTIAR

SERIES EDITOR
SEYYED HOSSEIN NASR

GREAT BOOKS OF THE ISLAMIC WORLD

Library of Congress Cataloging-in-Publication Data

Ḥujjat al-Islām Abū Ḥāmid Muḥammad Ghazzālī Ṭūsī (AH450/CE1059 to AH505/CE1111), commonly known as al-Ghazzali. *Al-Ghazzali On Disciplining the Self* from the *Alchemy of Happiness (Kimiya al-saadat),* the Persian translation by al-Ghazzali of the *Ihya ulum al-din (Revival of the Religious Sciences)*
1. Islamic psychology. 2. Sufism. 3. Islamic theology—Early works to 1800. 4. Ghazzali, 1058-1111. I. Title.

ISBN: 1-57644-693-0 pbk

Cover design: Liaquat Ali
Cornerstones are Allah and Muhammad connected by *Bismillāh al-Raḥmān al-Raḥīm* (In the Name of God, the Merciful, the Compassionate).

Logo design by Mani Ardalan Farhadi
The cypress tree bending with the wind, the source for the paisley design, is a symbol of the perfect Muslim, who, as the tree, bends with the wind of God's Will.

Published by
Great Books of the Islamic World, Inc.
Distributed by
KAZI Publications, Inc.
3023 W. Belmont Avenue
Chicago IL 60618
Tel: 773-267-7001; FAX: 773-267-7002
email: info@kazi.org /www.kazi.org

INTRODUCTION

". . . be not like those who forgot God and [eventually] God caused them to forget their 'self' . . . " (Q. 59:18-19)

There is nothing more timely today than a translation of the remarkable work on Islam of al-Ghazzali for two reasons. First of all, the results of recent studies of medicine-psychology and religious belief[1] confirm that the religious model works in the healing process so traditional wisdom must be made available in English for all researchers as well as readers to be able to access it and draw upon it for areas of further research. Secondly, at a time when the world is confused by the varying beliefs of Muslims and are interested in studying what the majority of the world's Muslims believe, the works of al-Ghazzali provide the perfect opportunity.

Abu Hamid Muhammad al-Ghazzali was born in the city of Tus, northwestern Iran, in AD 1058.[2] He studied in Tus until he was twenty-seven when he moved to Baghdad. He was appointed as a professor at the Nizamiyyah college there when he was thirty-three. After four years of a strenuous schedule, he underwent a spiritual experience which convinced him that all of the knowledge he had gained was useless in comparison to gnosis or experiential knowledge of the Divine Presence. He realized unless he left his position and was free to search for this knowledge deeper within himself without worldly distractions, he would never attain it. He therefore provided for his family and left for Damascus and other well known cities at that time.

When he was forty-eight he returned to his birthplace where he lived for the next five years until his early death at the age of fifty-three.[3] He left behind over 400 works among them being his famous *Revival of the Religious Sciences (Ihya ulum al-din)* which he wrote in Arabic. Over 2300 pages, it is a compendium of Islamic practices. A few years after he finished the *Revival*, he felt the need to write the same sort of compendium on being a Muslim in Persian. This is the entire work here translated into English for the first time which al-Ghazzali called the *Alchemy of Happiness*. It is a masterful textbook on traditional psychology.[4]

While modern Western psychology focuses on describing emotions, behavior or cognition, that is, what we feel, do and think without recourse to the basic principles or causes, traditional psychology is based on the same three centers, but like all traditional sciences, includes much more. As a result of including metaphysics, theology, cosmology and the natural sciences as the basis or underlying principles for what we feel, do or think, it becomes a wholistic psychology. The goal of traditional psychology is to assume the noble character traits, to overcome our ego which competes for our attention with our God-given instinct to attend to the One God. In this view, there cannot be two wills and therefore our free will has to be disciplined to submit to God's will *(islam)*.

The word psychology comes from the Greek words "psyche" or "soul" and "logos." Psyche also means breath, spirit and refers to the animating principle of the universe. Logos means "word" and in the traditional view it refers to "the Word of God." The science of psychology, then, when it is true to its name, is the study of the Word of God within the human soul or spirit.

Al-Ghazzali's psychology is essentially that of monotheism and unity, the world view that "there is no god, but God" or "there is no deity, but God." It is to see the universe and all that is in it as aspects of the One God. The world view of monotheism (*tawhid*) forms the underlying basis for traditional psychology.

By the word "tradition" we mean *al-din* which has been defined as: "truths or principles of a Divine Origin revealed or unveiled to mankind through a messenger along with the ramifications and application of these principles in different realms including law, social structure, art, symbols, the sciences and embracing Supreme Knowledge along with the means for its attainment."[5]

Tradition (*al-din*) is a point which is at one and the same time the Center and Origin of our being. Traditional psychology is oriented towards helping the individual as well as the human community find that Center as we prepare for the return to our Origin.

A monotheist (*hanif*) like al-Ghazzali regards the whole universe as a unity, as a single form, a single living and conscious thing, possessing will, intelligence, feeling, and purpose, revolving in a just and orderly system in which there is no discrimination no matter what one's gender, color, race, class, or faith be. All comes from God and returns to God, while a multitheist (*mushrik*) views the universe as a discordant assemblage full of disunity, contradiction, and heterogeneity containing many independent and conflicting poles, unconnected desires, customs, purposes, wills, sexes, sects, colors, races, classes, and faiths.

The monotheistic world view sees the universal unity in existence, a unity of three separate relationships: (1) our relationship with others, nature and the universe; (2) our relationship with God; (3) our relationship with our "self." These relationships are not alien to one another; there are no bound-

aries between them. They move in the same direction. Al-
Ghazzali expresses this when he writes:

> Then know that there is a station in gnosis
> (*marifat*) where, when a person reaches it, he real-
> ly sees that all that exists is interconnectedness,
> one with another, and all are like one animate
> being. The relationship of the parts of the world
> such as the heavens, the earth, the stars to each
> other is like the relationship of the parts of one ani-
> mate being to each other. The relationship of all the
> world to its Director—from one aspect, not from all
> aspects—is like the relationship of the kingdom of
> the body of an animal to the spirit and intellect
> which are its Director. Until a person recognizes
> this, that Verily, God created Adam in His image, it
> cannot be comprehended by his understanding."[6]

Other non-monotheistic religious world views see the
Divinity—or even the plural of this—as existing in a special,
metaphysical world of the gods, a higher world as contrasted
with the lower world of nature and matter. They teach that
God is separate from the world, created it and then left it
alone. In the monotheistic world view, God has never left and
is the destination of the Return. In this view, our "self" fears
only one Power and is answerable to only one Judge; turns to
one direction (*qiblah*), orienting all hopes and desires to only
one Source. A belief in monotheism gives us a sense of inde-
pendence and liberation from everything other than God and
a connectedness to the universe and all that it contains.
Submission to God's Will alone liberates us from worshipping
anything other than God and rebelling against anything else
that purports to be God.

AL-GHAZZALI'S THREE FUNDAMENTALS

Al-Ghazzali sees the basis for traditional psychology lead-

ing to self-development as consisting of three fundamentals—
the same three fundamentals confirmed by modern psychology and scientific studies—affect, behavior and cognition (the ABC of psychology). The first fundamental is knowledge (cognition, awareness or consciousness). The second he calls states (affect or emotion) that that knowledge or awareness produces in us. The third he calls act or deed— the action that results from our emotion that came from our knowledge or awareness of something.

THE FIRST FUNDAMENTAL: KNOWLEDGE (COGNITION)

According to al-Ghazzali, knowledge should be used to come to understand the articles of belief rather than accepting them on faith alone. The articles of belief include: the belief that God is One; the belief that God sent Prophets to guide mankind to Him and that Muhammad is the Messenger and last Prophet who will be sent (until the end of time when Jesus will return) and that the Quran is the last revelation; the belief in angels and the Scriptures; and the belief that after death we will be resurrected in the Hereafter and judged by God who will reward or punish us depending upon our intentions. Al-Ghazzali says: "It is the states of the heart, the place of our intentions, that holds us accountable."[7]

BELIEFS

Our beliefs are the guiding principles that give meaning and direction to our life. They filter our perceptions of the world. When we freely choose to believe something is true, a command is delivered to our spiritual heart (mind) telling us how to represent what we have come to believe to be true. When the process has been accomplished with Divine Grace (defined by al-Ghazzali as: the harmony, agreement and concord of our will and action with God's will), our beliefs can become our most effective force for creating the positive and good in our lives.

In explaining the importance of coming to the realization of the Oneness of God oneself and not accepting it because someone has told us, al-Ghazzali says:

> Know that the first duty incumbent upon whoever becomes a Muslim is to know and believe the meaning of the utterance "there is no god but God, Muhammad is the Messenger of God," which he pronounces with his tongue, understands in his heart, and believes so that he entertains no doubt about it. When he has believed and his heart is established firmly upon (that belief)—so that doubt cannot touch it—it is sufficient for the basis of being (one who submits to God's Will (*muslim*)). Knowing it with evidence and proof is an individual duty incumbent upon every (one who submits to God's Will (*muslim*)). The Prophet did not command the Arabs to seek proofs, to study theology, or to look for doubts and replies to those; rather, he was content with belief and faith.[8]

He then defines what belief in submission to God's Will (*islam*) means:

> Know that you have been created and that you have a Creator Who is the Creator of all the universe and all that it contains. He is One. He has no partner nor associate. He is Unique, for He has no peer. He always was; His existence has no beginning. He always shall be; there is no end to His existence. His existence in eternity and infinity is a necessary, for annihilation cannot touch Him. His existence is by His own essence. He needs nothing but nothing is unneedful of Him. Rather, He is estab-

lished by His Own essence, and everything else is established through Him.[9]

Al-Ghazzali mentions five sources for our beliefs:

(1) Our environment: how we grow up; models of success or failure we learn from; what is right and what is wrong; what is possible and what is impossible.

(2) Our experiences and events as we grow up.

(3) Knowledge: what we know and do not know; that we continue to educate our "self" from "the cradle to the grave."

(4) Results we have seen achieved in the past, learned from the stories of past people in the Quran.

(5) Setting new goals to achieve future results.

Future results depend upon how we incorporate our beliefs—how we view the world—into our own self image. According to al-Ghazzali, our firm and certain belief in the Oneness of God should lead us—as it did Prophet Muhammad—to the following beliefs:

(i) The belief that everything happens for a reason. We look for the good and positive in whatever happens.

(ii) The belief that there is no such thing as failure, only results or outcomes. If we are able to train a falcon to hunt for us, al-Ghazzali uses as an example, we can train and discipline our rational faculty to control our passions. Al-Ghazzali says that we should not expect immediate results. Change is gradual. We need to develop patience, a great virtue in his view.

(iii) The belief that we must take responsibility for whatever happens. No matter what happens, know and believe that we are in charge. The Prophet never blamed others for whatever happened. He never allowed himself to be a victim. As the Quran says: *"God does not change the condition of a people until they change what is within themselves."* (Q. 13:11)

(iv) The belief that we need to learn from other people who

are our greatest resource. Treat them with respect and dignity as the Prophet did.

(v) The belief that we need to challenge our profession or line of work and excel in it. Explore new ways of doing things. Increase our sense of curiosity and vitality.

(vi) The belief that there is no success without commitment. Know our outcome in the Hereafter as the Prophet knew. Develop our sensory responses so we know what we are getting and then continue to refine it until we get what we want. Study the key beliefs of the Prophet and then hold tight to them.

In al-Ghazzali's view, if we firmly believe we are among those "who submit to God's Will" (*muslim*), then with our cognition, affect and behavior as understood from the monotheistic point of view as our foundation, we can submit in everything that we say or do. What we believe to be true becomes possible when we know what we want—to be one who submits to God's will—and believe we can achieve it.

STRATEGIES

Developing a strategy is to duplicate our belief system. When we organize the way we think, the way we feel and the way we behave according to our belief system, we have developed a strategy. The ingredients of our strategy are our human experiences. Our experiences are fed from our five outer senses: seeing, smelling, hearing, tasting and touching. Our five senses motivate us to action. When we are aware of what they perceive and keep their perceptions in line with our belief system, we have developed a successful strategy.

The amounts we use of the information provided by our senses is monitored by our spiritual heart (mind). Are the images small or large, bright or unclear, close up or far away? How we put these together, their order and sequence clarifies our strategy.

With our resource being our "self" consisting of body, spirit, soul and spiritual heart (it is our spiritual heart that centers us), we want to learn what we need to do to organize this resource. How can we have our goal and belief achieve the greatest potential? What is the most effective way to use the resource of our "self" and its subparts? The most effective strategy has always been modeling the behavior of others who have the same goal and the same belief. For the believer, this model is that of the Messenger Muhammad who was the perfect human being.

Strategies he used included performing the prescribed fast as well as formal prayer, supplication and continuous recitation of the revelation. For the believer, revelation brought both a Law and a Way. Both serve as strategies of how to approach life in the manner in which the model approached life, and knowing that our model did not always do things exactly the same way.

The strategy of Quranic recitation is yet another form of discipline. One of the verses of the Quran: *"Remember Me and I will remember you,"* (Q. 2:152) makes this form of supplication a very rich traditional strategy to attain spiritual energy.

THE SECOND FUNDAMENTAL: STATES
(AFFECT, EMOTION)

Our belief establishes states (emotions, affect) which then result in our actions. In this relationship and all others, our state of mind is
important because that determines our emotion and our emotion determines how many resources are available to us. Our emotions depend upon how we feel physically—our breathing, posture, etc.— and how we represent the world to ourselves internally. When we have cleared our spiritual heart of hypocrisy in our acts of worship, our actions are to worship

God and we are at the beginning stages of the greater struggle according to al-Ghazzali.

States (affect, emotion) are held or transformed in terms of psychology through moral values that energize us. Our behavior is the result of the state we are in at the time. Our emotional state governors our behavior. Behavior is the result of how we represent the information from our senses internally as well as our muscular tension, posture, physiology.

We have the resources we need to succeed. We have to learn how to access them. We need to learn to take direct control: Once we learn to manage our states (emotions), according to al-Ghazzali, we can modify our behavior. There is a difference of how people react to the same state. The difference depends on their model.

One of the best methods which al-Ghazzali uses over and over again in the *Alchemy* is that of what is today called reframing: changing the way we evaluate what something means. If our culture teaches us that change is a failure of opportunity for learning, we need to become resourceful, to realize that nothing has power over us but the power we give it by our own conscious thoughts. The meaning of any experience depends on the frame we put around it. If we change the context or reference point, the process changes.

We can reframe by context reframing or content reframing. With context reframing, we take a bad experience and show it in another way. With content reframing, we drastically change how we see, hear, or represent a situation. We learn to change the way we represent a situation so we feel differently about it. Now we are at the level of choice instead of reaction. By learning to reframe, we change our emotions so that they empower us. We can either associate or disassociate. If we associate consciously, we learn to change the way we represent things, thereby changing our behavior. We have to aim for congruence between our spiritual heart (mind) and body.

CLARITY OF MORAL VALUES

Clarity of values gives us a sense of who we are and why we do what we do. If we have an internal conflict between our values and our strategy, we will not succeed. Values determine what really matters in life. They provide us with a basis from which to make sound judgments about what makes life worth living.

Al-Ghazzali refers to verses 23:1-10 of the Quran as an example of believers who have succeeded by incorporating Quranic values:

> Certainly will the believers have succeeded: They who during their prayer humbly submissive; those who turn away from ill speech; they who are observant of the poor-due; they who guard their private parts except from their wives and those their right hands possess for indeed, they will not be blamed, but whatever seeks beyond that, then they are the transgressors; and they who are to their trusts and their promises attentive; and they who carefully maintain their prayers. Those are the inheritors. (Q. 23:1-10)

Al-Ghazzali then summarizes the verses to describe a person of good character.

> A person of good character is he who is modest, says little, causes little trouble, speaks the truth, seeks the good, worships much, has few faults, meddles little, desires the good for all, and does good works for all. He is compassionate, dignified, measured, patient, content, grateful, sympathetic, friendly, abstinent, and not greedy. He does not use foul language, nor does he exhibit haste, nor does he harbor hatred in his heart. He is not envious. He is candid, well-spoken, and his friendship and

enmity, his anger and his pleasure are for the sake
of God Most High and nothing more.[10]

In the *Alchemy* (as well as in the *Revival*), al-Ghazzali
devotes the major part of the work to clarity of moral values
by describing in great detail what he calls the Destroyers and
the Deliverers. He not only describes them in each of those
parts, but offers treatment as to how to get rid of them (the
Destroyers) or how to incorporate them into our personality
(the Deliverers). Doing this clarifies the moral values of the
one who submits to God's Will.

As a result of the performance of the acts of worship, if
accompanied by Divine Grace, the one who submits to the Will
of God will be receptive to the adoption of positive dispositions
(the deliverers) like temperance, courage, wisdom, and justice
and be able to avoid negative dispositions (the destroyers) like
anger, fear of other than God, cowardice, lust, envy, apathy,
preconsciousness (knowing that you do not know), uncon-
sciousness (not knowing that you do not know) and overcon-
sciousness (knowing but deceiving the self about it), but only
on the condition that others benefit from the positive dispositions one has attained. This, then, makes it encumbent on the
one who has submitted to the Will of God to come to know and
act upon the commands that underlie the relationship of self
to others.

ENERGY

The entire human organism is a complete system that
makes use of energy transformed from food and air to satisfy
its various natural dispositions. Perception (external and
internal senses) and motivation develop, according to traditional psychology, from the animal soul. Motivation is the seat
of impulses towards inclinations which are imprinted on the
external or internal senses and then, through filtering into

what is called the practical intellect (the mind), a response is given. Three energy sources are active in this perspective: natural (venial, *tabiiya*), vital (arterial, *nafsaniyah*), and nervous (*hawaniyah*). These transformed energies are distributed throughout the body. The heart is considered to be the point of contact between the energy of the body and that of the self.

Without the necessary energy, which according to al-Ghazzali comes from spiritual practices, we reach a state of hoplessness and despair. For instance, if someone asked: "If one has been condemned to hardship, what is the benefit of the greater struggle?" Al-Ghazzali explains this attitude:

> Your question is valid. These words are correct in that they are the cause of the illness of our heart. That is, when a sign of a concept that a person has been condemned to hardship falls upon his heart, they cause him to make no effort, neither sowing nor reaping. Such a sign would be when a person who has been condemned to death becomes hungry the thought occurs in his heart not to eat. He says: "What good is bread to me?" He does not extend his hand to eat and he does not eat until by necessity he dies. If he has been condemned to poverty, he says: "Of what use is sowing seed?" so he neither sows nor reaps. And he for whom happiness has been decreed, he has been made aware that wealth and life have been decreed for him. They have been decreed because he has cultivated, done business, and consumed. Therefore, this decree is not invalid; rather it has reasons"[11]

THE THIRD FUNDAMENTAL: ACTIONS (BEHAVIOR)

Knowledge alone is not sufficient for we who accepted the trusteeship of nature and were endowed with the Divine Spirit which includes our abilities to choose, to discern, and to gain consciousness of our "self." It is through actions based on knowledge that the centered self benefits another as proof of being centered. The major pillars include ritual purity (*taharah*) and ritual prayer (*salah*), ritual fast (*saum*), the paying of the alms tax (*zakah*), the pilgrimage (*hajj*), counseling to positive dispositions and preventing the development of negative ones (*amr bil maruf wa nahy an al-munkar*) and *jihad* or struggle in the Way of God, the greater struggle of which is the inward struggle of the self (*jihad al-akbar*). The last two are the major concern of traditional psychology.

BONDING POWER OR RAPPORT

Bonding and communicating are aspects of action—proof of the extent of transformation through attaining the goal that we had intended. The power to bond with others is an extraordinary human power. It comes in the true sense when bonding develops from the heart and not from either the intellect or the passions. It comes from a deep love for one's fellow human being and arises when we try to meet the needs of others before our own needs, much like a mother with her new born child.

Al-Ghazzali quoting from the Quran, the Prophet and the Companions mentions how important it is to eat with other people and to perform the formal obligatory prayer with other people.

COMMUNICATORS

Believers should conceivably be master communicators on all three levels—with self, with others and with the Source. How we communicate determines the quality of our lives. Through spiritual disciplines like, for example, prescribed fasting, believers are given an opportunity, a challenge. If they are able to communicate that challenge to themselves successfully, they will find the ability to change. This is not to accept prescribed fasting as only a religious duty but rather as a divine challenge, as a chance for growth instead of an experience which limits self. In this way we will become master communicators because our very life will communicate our vision, goal and beliefs to others to help them change for the better, as well.

RELATIONSHIP TO OTHERS

Al-Ghazzali discusses knowledge (cognition), states (affect) and action (behavior) in three relationships: our relationship with others; our relationship with our Creator-Guide; and our relationship with our "self."

The model for this is the *sunnah* of Muhammad who said, "I was sent to complete the noble qualities of dispositions," explaining that God loves the positive dispositions and not the negative ones. Al-Ghazzali also quotes another Tradition in this regard, "By Him in whose hand is my life, no one shall enter paradise except the one who has positive dispositions." Al-Ghazzali says, "God taught [Muhammad all the fine qualities of disposition, praiseworthy paths, reports about the first and last affairs, and matters through which one achieves salvation and reward in future life and happiness and reward in the world to come."

Quoting the Traditions, al-Ghazzali shows the relationship established by the Prophet with others.

> And the Messenger said: "There are not two persons who love each other for the sake of God that the one most beloved by God is the one loves the other the most." And he said: "God Most High says: 'My love is a right for those who visit one another for My sake, who love each other for My sake, who are generous to each other with their wealth for My

sake, and who aid each other for My sake.'" And he said: "On the Day of Resurrection God Most High will say: 'Where are those persons who loved each other for My sake so that I may keep them in My shadow on this day when there is no shade for the people in which to take refuge?'" And he said: "There are seven persons on the Day of Resurrection who, when there will be no shade for anyone, will be in the shadow of God Most High: the just leader (imam), the young person who began worshipping God Most High at the beginning of his youth, the man who leaves the mosque with his heart attached to the mosque until he returns to it again, two people who love each other for the sake of God Most High and who come together for that and separate for that, the person who remembers God Most High in private and whose eyes fill with tears, and the man who when called by a magnificent and beautiful woman says to her: 'I fear God Most High,' and the man who gives voluntary charity with his right hand so that the left hand has knowledge of it." And he said: "No one visits a brother for the sake of God Most High save that an angel cries out, saying: 'Be happy and blessed! Thine is the heaven of God Most High!'"

And he said: "A man was going to visit a friend. God Most High sent an angel in his path who asked: 'Where are you going?' He replied: 'To visit such-and-such a brother.' (The angel) asked: 'Do you have some business with him?' He said: 'No.' (The angel) asked: 'Are you related to him in some way?' He said: 'No.' (The angel) asked: 'Has he done something good for you?' He answered: 'No.' (The angel) said: 'Then why are you going to him?' He answered: 'I love him for the sake of God.' (The angel) said: 'Then, God Most High has sent me to you to give you the good news that God Most High loves you because of your love for him, and has made heaven an obligation for both of you yourselves.'" And the Messenger said: "The strongest resort of faith is love and enmity for the sake of God Most High."[12]

Al-Ghazzali describes relationships with others ranking them in degrees.

The first degree is that you love someone for some reason linked with him, but that motive is religious and for the sake of God Most High; as you like your teacher because he teaches you knowledge. That friendship is of a divine nature since your aim for (acquiring) this knowledge is the Hereafter, not rank or wealth. If the object be the world, that friendship is not of that kind. If you love your student so that he learn from you and may obtain the pleasure of God Most High through learning, (you) too obtain the spiritual reward of teaching. This is for the sake of God Most High. But if you love (him) for the sake of dignity and retinue, it will not be of that kind. If a person gives voluntary charity and likes a person on the condition that he deliver that to the poor; or he invites some poor people and likes a person who prepares a good meal, then such friendship is for the sake of God. Indeed, if one likes someone and gives him bread and clothing to give him the leisure to worship (God), it is friendship for the sake of God, since his motive is the peace of mind for worship.

Many religious scholars and worshippers have had friendships with the rich and powerful for this reason. Both were counted as friends for the sake of God Most High. Moreover, if one loves his own wife because she keeps him from corruption and because of the bringing forth of children who will supplicate for him, such love is for the sake of God Most High and everything you spent for her is a voluntary charity. Indeed, if one loves his student for two rea-

sons: one that he serves him and the other that he
gives him the peace of mind to perform his worship,
that part which is for worship is counted as love for
the sake of God most High and there is spiritual
reward for it.

The second degree is greater. It is that one love
a person for the sake of God without having any
expectations from him; instead, it is by reason of
obedience to God and for the love of Him that he
loves the other. Moreover, because he is a servant of
God and created by Him—such friendship is divine.
It is greater because this arises from the excess of
one's love of God Most High, so much so that it
reaches the boundaries of passionate love. Whoever
is in love with someone, loves (that person's) district
and neighborhood. He loves the walls of (that person's) house; indeed, he loves the dog roaming the
quarter's streets, and he likes that dog more than
other (dogs). He is compelled to love the friend of
his beloved, and beloved of his beloved, the people
who obey the commands of his beloved; (the
beloved's) servants, captives, or relatives; all of
these he loves out of necessity, for his love spreads
to whatever has a relation with his beloved. As his
love increases so it does with the others who follow
and are connected with the beloved.[13]

ESTABLISHING THE RELATIONSHIP
BETWEEN THE SELF AND OUR CREATOR-GUIDE

This relationship is established, according to al-Ghazzali,
through the commands of worship (*ibadah*), which are the
most fundamental means of communication between our "self"
and God. They embody the same three aspects: knowledge
(cognition), states (affect, process) and action (behavior). One
who submits to the Will of God seeks knowledge of particular
guidance. This produces a "state" (emotion) in the self which

then responds with an action as al-Ghazzali explains:

> Know that object and kernel of all acts of wor-
> ship are the remembrance of God Most High; that
> the buttress of Islam is obligatory formal prayer,
> the object of which is the remembrance of God Most
> High. As He said: *Surely (formal) prayer prevents*
> *lewdness and evil, and indeed the remembrance of*
> *God is greater (than all else)*. (Q. 29:45)
>
> Reading the Quran is the most meritorious of
> the acts of worship, for the reason that it is the
> word of God Most High: (reading or reciting it) is
> remembering Him. Everything that is in it all cause
> a renewal of the remembrance of God, may He be
> praised and exalted. The object of fasting is the
> reduction of the carnal appetite so that the heart,
> liberated from the annoyance of the carnal
> appetites, becomes purified and the abode of
> remembrance; for when the heart is filled with car-
> nal appetite, it is not possible to remember (Him);
> nor does (the remembrance) affect one. The object of
> the greater pilgrimage, which is a visit to the House
> of God, is the remembrance of the Lord of that
> House and the incitement of longing for meeting
> Him.
>
> Thus the inner mystery and the kernel of all of
> the acts of worship are remembrance. Indeed, the
> basis of Islam is the declaration: "there is no god
> but God"; this is the source of remembrance. All
> other acts of worship stress this remembrance.
> God's remembrance of you is the fruit of your
> remembrance of Him; what fruit could be greater
> than this? For this He said: *So remember Me, I shall*
> *remember you*. (Q. 2:152)
>
> This remembrance must be continuous. If it is
> not continuous, it should be most of the time; for
> salvation is tied to it. For this He said: *And remem-*
> *ber God much; perhaps you will be successful*. (Q.
> 62:10) He says that if you have the hope of salva-

tion, the key to that is much remembrance, not a little, and more frequently, not less.

And for this He said: *Those who remember God standing, sitting, and lying down.* (Q. 3:191) He praised these people because they do not neglect (remembrance) standing, sitting, lying down, or in any condition. And He said: *Remember thy Lord, (O Muhammad), within thyself humbly and with awe, in a soft voice, in the morning and in the evening, and be not of the neglectful.* (Q. 7:205) He said: "*Remember Him with weeping, fear, and in concealment, morning and evening, and do not neglect (this) at any time.*"

The Messenger was asked: "What is the best of acts?" He answered: "That you die with your tongue moist with the remembrance of God Most High." And he said: "Should I not inform you of the best of your actions—the most acceptable to the King, may He be exalted—and your highest degrees, that which is better than giving alms of silver and gold, and better than shedding your blood in battle against enemies in defense of the faith?" They asked: "What is that, O Messenger of God?" He said: "The remembrance of God." The remembrance of God Most High! And he said: "Whoever remembering me engages in worshipful supplication of God, his gift is, in my opinion, greater and better than giving (charity) to beggars." And he said: "The rememberer of God Most High among the heedless is like a living person amongst the dead, or like a green tree amongst dead vegetation, or like the warrior for the faith who stands fighting amongst those fleeing. . .[14] In summary, the strength of one's love for God Most High is in accordance with the strength of one's faith. The stronger one's faith, the more overwhelming one's love is.[15]

KNOW YOUR "SELF"

The most important relationship for the purposes of traditional psychology is that of our relationship to our "self." Our "self" as we have seen, consists of body, spirit, soul and spiritual heart. We turn now to the *Alchemy*'s Prolegomena (added here by al-Ghazzali, it does not appear in the *Revival*) where al-Ghazzali explores how to come to know the "self" in great detail.

*****

The traditional method of teaching a text is for the teacher to read it part by part with a class of students and then comment on what the text is saying. This is the method used next taking just the first subsection of Topic One of the Prolegomena, "Knowing Yourself" which appears in the following paragraphs in bold. The commentary and explanations that follow are enhanced with other sections of al-Ghazzali's writings in the *Alchemy* which are inset for clarity. If we were sitting in al-Ghazzali's classroom, this is the method he would be using.

NOTES TO THE INTRODUCTION

1 See works like *Timeless Healing: The Power and Biology of Belief* by Herbert Benson; *Why God Won't Go Away: Brain Science and the Biology of Belief* by Andrew Newberg, Eugene D'Aquili and Vince Rause; and *Handbook of Religion and Health* edited by Harold G. Koniz, Michael McCullough and David B. Larsen.

2 Other well known writers and poets born in Tus include Abu Yazid Bistami, Husayn bin Mansur Hallaj, Abu Said Abi'l-Khayr, Nizam al-Mulk, Firdawsi and Umar Khayyam.

3 See Bibliography to the Introduction for the numerous books that detail the life of al-Ghazzali. It is interesting to note that al-Ghazzali wrote the *Alchemy of Happiness* when the First Crusade ruled Jerusalem. Saladin arrived on the scene seventy-seven years after al-Ghazzali's death.

4 See below for the definition of traditional psychology which historically was called the science of ethics or practical wisdom (*hikmat al-amali*).

5 *Knowledge and the Sacred*, p. 68.

6 *Alchemy*, p. 841.

7 This is a clear distinction with modern secular psychology which is limited to only treating a human being part by part instead of holistically. See *Alchemy* p 817.

8 *Alchemy*, p 358.

9 *Alchemy,* p. 116.

10 *Alchemy*, p 525.

11 *Alchemy*, p 780.

12 *Alchemy*, p 358.

13 *Alchemy*, p 360.

14 *Alchemy*, pp 221-222.

15 *Ibid.*

BIBLIOGRAPHY

al-Ghazzali. *Alchemy of Happiness* abridged. Translated by Claud Field. Lahore: Sh. Muhammad Ashraf, 1987. 1100 pages summarized in 60 pages.

al-Ghazzali. *Alchemy of Happiness.* Complete translation by Jay R. Crook. Chicago: Kazi Publications, 2002.

al-Ghazzali. *Confessions.* Translated by Claud Field. Lahore: Sh. Muhammad Ashraf, 1992.

al-Ghazzali. *Deliverance from Error.* Translated by R. J. McCarthy. KY: fons vitae, 1980.

al-Ghazzali. *Faith in Divine Unity and Trust in Divine Providence.* Translated from the *Ihya ulum al-din (Kitab al-tawhid wa'l tawakkul).* Translated by David B. Burrell. Cambridge: Islamic Texts Society, 2001.

al-Ghazzali. *Ihya ulum al-din (Revival of the Religious Sciences).* Translated by al-Hajj Maulana Fazul ul-Karim. Lahore: Islamic Publications Bureau, n.d.

al-Ghazzali, *Incoherence of the Philosophers.* Translated by Michael E. Marmura. A parallel English-Arabic text. Provo, Utah: Brigham University Press, 1952.

al-Ghazzali. *Inner Dimensions of Islamic Worship.* Translated from the *Ihya ulum al-din.* Leicester; Islamic Foundation, 1990.

al-Ghazzali. *Invocations and Supplications.* Translated from the *Ihya ulum al-din (Kitab al-adhkar wal daawat)* by K. Nakamura. Cambridge: Islamic Texts Society, 1996.

al-Ghazzali, *Just Balance (al-Qistas al-mustaqim),* Translated by D. P. Brewster. Lahore, Pakistan: Sh. Muhammad Ashraf, 1987.

al-Ghazzali. *Letters of al-Ghazzali.* Translated by Abdul Qayyum. Lahore: Islamic Publications (Pvt), Ltd. , 1994.

al-Ghazzali. *Mishkat al-anwar.* Translated by W. H. T. Gairdner. Lahore: Sh. Muhammad Ashraf, 1991.

al-Ghazzali. *Mysteries of Almsgiving.* Translated from the *Ihya ulum al-din (Kitab asrar al-zakah)* by Nabih Amin Faris. Lahore: Sh. Muhammad Ashraf, 1992.

al-Ghazzali, *Mysteries of Fasting.* Translated from the *Ihya ulum al-din* by Nabih Amin Faris. Lahore: Sh. Muhammad Ashraf, 1992.

al-Ghazzali. *Mysteries of Purity.* Translated from the *Ihya ulum al-din* by Nabih Amir Faris. Lahore: Sh. Muhammad Ashraf, 1991.

al-Ghazzali. *Mysteries of Worship.* Translated from the *Ihya ulum al-din* by Edwin Elliot Calverley. Lahore: Sh. Muhammad Ashraf, 1998.

al-Ghazzali, *Niche of Lights.* Translated by David Buchman. A parallel English-Arabic text. Provo, Utah: Brigham university Press, 1998.

al-Ghazzali. *Ninety-nine Beautiful Names of God (al-Maqsad al-asna fi sharh asma Allah al-husna)*. Translated by David B. Burrell and Nazih Daher. Cambridge: Islamic Texts Society, 1999.

Al-Ghazzali On Disciplining the Self. Translated from the *Alchemy of Happiness* by Muhammad Nur Abdus Salam (Jay R. Crook). Chicago: Kazi Publications, 2002.

al-Ghazzali. *On Disciplining the Soul and the Two Desires.* Translated from the *Ihya ulum al-din (Kitab riyadat al-nafs. Kitab kasr al-shahwatayn)* by T. J. Winter. Cambridge: Islamic Texts Society, 2001.

al-Ghazzali. *On Divine Predicates and their Properties (al-Iqtisad fil'itiqad).* Translated by Abdu Rahman Abu Zayd. India: Kitab Bhavan, 1994.

Al-Ghazzali On Earning a Living and Trade. Translated from *Alchemy of Happiness* by Muhammad Nur Abdus Salam (Jay R. Crook). Chicago: Kazi Publications, 2002.

Al-Ghazzali On Enjoining Good and Forbidding Wrong. Translated from *Alchemy of Happiness* by Muhammad Nur Abdus Salam (Jay R. Crook). Chicago: Kazi Publications, 2002.

Al-Ghazzali On Governing and Managing the State. Translated from *Alchemy of Happiness* by Muhammad Nur Abdus Salam (Jay R. Crook). Chicago: Kazi Publications, 2002.

Al-Ghazzali On Hope and Fear. Translated from *Alchemy of Happiness* by Muhammad Nur Abdus Salam (Jay R. Crook). Chicago: Kazi Publications, 2002.

Al-Ghazzali On Journeying. Translated from *Alchemy of Happiness* by Muhammad Nur Abdus Salam (Jay R. Crook). Chicago: Kazi Publications, 2002.

Al-Ghazzali On Knowing This World and the Hereafter. Translated from *Alchemy of Happiness* by Muhammad Nur Abdus Salam (Jay R. Crook). Chicago: Kazi Publications, 2002.

Al-Ghazzali On Knowing Yourself and God. Translated from *Alchemy of Happiness* by Muhammad Nur Abdus Salam (Jay R. Crook). Chicago: Kazi Publications, 2002.

Al-Ghazzali On Listening to Music. Translated from *Alchemy of Happiness* by Muhammad Nur Abdus Salam (Jay R. Crook). Chicago: Kazi Publications, 2002.

Al-Ghazzali On Love, Longing and Contentment. Translated from *Alchemy of Happiness* by Muhammad Nur Abdus Salam (Jay R. Crook). Chicago: Kazi Publications, 2002.

Al-Ghazzali On Marriage. Translated from *Alchemy of Happiness* by Muhammad Nur Abdus Salam (Jay R. Crook). Chicago: Kazi Publications, 2002.

Al-Ghazzali On Meditation. Translated from *Alchemy of Happiness* by Muhammad Nur Abdus Salam (Jay R. Crook). Chicago: Kazi

Publications, 2002.

Al-Ghazzali On Patience and Gratitude. Translated from *Alchemy of Happiness* by Muhammad Nur Abdus Salam (Jay R. Crook). Chicago: Kazi Publications, 2002.

Al-Ghazzali On Reckoning and Guarding. Translated from *Alchemy of Happiness* by Muhammad Nur Abdus Salam (Jay R. Crook). Chicago: Kazi Publications, 2002.

Al-Ghazzali On Remembering Death and the States of the Hereafter. Translated from *Alchemy of Happiness* by Muhammad Nur Abdus Salam (Jay R. Crook). Chicago: Kazi Publications, 2002.

Al-Ghazzali On Repentance. Translated from *Alchemy of Happiness* by Muhammad Nur Abdus Salam (Jay R. Crook). Chicago: Kazi Publications, 2002.

Al-Ghazzali On Spiritual Poverty and Asceticism. Translated from *Alchemy of Happiness* by Muhammad Nur Abdus Salam (Jay R. Crook). Chicago: Kazi Publications, 2002.

Al-Ghazzali On Sufism. Translated from *Alchemy of Happiness* by Muhammad Nur Abdus Salam (Jay R. Crook). Chicago: Kazi Publications, 2002.

Al-Ghazzali On the Duties of Brotherhood. Translated from *Alchemy of Happiness* by Muhammad Nur Abdus Salam (Jay R. Crook). Chicago: Kazi Publications, 2002.

Al-Ghazzali On the Etiquette of Eating. Translated from *Alchemy of Happiness* by Muhammad Nur Abdus Salam (Jay R. Crook). Chicago: Kazi Publications, 2002.

al-Ghazzali. *On the Foundations of the Articles of Faith.* Translated from the *Ihya ulum al-din* (*Kitab qawaid al-aqaid*) by Nabih Amir Faris. Lahore: Sh. Muhammad Ashraf, 1999.

Al-Ghazzali On the Lawful, the Unlawful and the Doubtful. Translated from *Alchemy of Happiness* by Muhammad Nur Abdus Salam (Jay R. Crook). Chicago: Kazi Publications, 2002.

al-Ghazzali. *On the Manners Relating to Eating.* Translated from the *Ihya ulum al-din* (*Kitab adab al-akl*) by D. Johnson-Davies. Cambridge: Islamic Texts Society, 2000.

Al-Ghazzali On the Mysteries of the Pillars of Islam. Translated from *Alchemy of Happiness* by Muhammad Nur Abdus Salam (Jay R. Crook). Chicago: Kazi Publications, 2002.

Al-Ghazzali On the Treatment of Anger, Hatred and Envy. Translated from *Alchemy of Happiness* by Muhammad Nur Abdus Salam (Jay R. Crook). Chicago: Kazi Publications, 2002.

Al-Ghazzali On the Treatment of Hypocrisy. Translated from *Alchemy of Happiness* by Muhammad Nur Abdus Salam (Jay R. Crook). Chicago: Kazi Publications, 2002.

Al-Ghazzali On the Treatment of Ignorance Arising from Heedlessness, Error and Delusion. Translated from *Alchemy of Happiness* by Muhammad Nur Abdus Salam (Jay R. Crook). Chicago: Kazi Publications, 2002.

Al-Ghazzali On the Treatment of Love for This World. Translated from *Alchemy of Happiness* by Muhammad Nur Abdus Salam (Jay R. Crook). Chicago: Kazi Publications, 2002.

Al-Ghazzali On the Treatment of Love of Power and Control. Translated from *Alchemy of Happiness* by Muhammad Nur Abdus Salam (Jay R. Crook). Chicago: Kazi Publications, 2002.

Al-Ghazzali On the Treatment of Miserliness and Greed. Translated from *Alchemy of Happiness* by Muhammad Nur Abdus Salam (Jay R. Crook). Chicago: Kazi Publications, 2002.

Al-Ghazzali On the Treatment of Pride and Conceit. Translated from *Alchemy of Happiness* by Muhammad Nur Abdus Salam (Jay R. Crook). Chicago: Kazi Publications, 2002.

Al-Ghazzali On the Treatment of the Harms of the Tongue. Translated from *Alchemy of Happiness* by Muhammad Nur Abdus Salam (Jay R. Crook). Chicago: Kazi Publications, 2002.

Al-Ghazzali On the Treatment of the Lust of the Stomach and the Sexual Organs. Translated from *Alchemy of Happiness* by Muhammad Nur Abdus Salam (Jay R. Crook). Chicago: Kazi Publications, 2002.

Al-Ghazzali On Trust and the Unity of God. Translated from *Alchemy of Happiness* by Muhammad Nur Abdus Salam (Jay R. Crook). Chicago: Kazi Publications, 2002.

Al-Ghazzali On Truthfulness and Sincerity. Translated from *Alchemy of Happiness* by Muhammad Nur Abdus Salam (Jay R. Crook). Chicago: Kazi Publications, 2002.

Avicenna. *The Canon of Medicine*. Chicago: Kazi Publications, 1999.

Benson, Herbert. *Timeless Healing: The Power and Biology of Belief*. NY: Simon and Schuster, 1996.

Ethical Philosophy of al-Ghazzali. Muhammad Umar ud-Din. Lahore: Sh. Muhammad Ashraf, 1991.

Faith and Practice of al-Ghazzali. W. Montgomery Watt. Edinburgh: Edinburgh University Press, 1952. An abridged translation of *Munqidh min ad-dalal* (Deliverance from Error) and the Beginning of Guidance (*Bidayat al-hidayah*).

Fakhry, Majid. *Al-Ghazzali's Theory of Virtue*. NY: SUNY, 1985.

Koniz, Harold G., Michael McCullough and David B. Larsen. *Handbook of Religion and Health*. NY: Oxford University Press, 2001.

Newberg, Andrew, Eugene D'Aquili and Vince Rause. *Why God Won't Go Away: Brain Science and the Biology of Belief*. NY: Ballantine Books, 2002.

AL-GHAZZALI
ON DISCIPLINING THE SELF

In this Book we shall discuss the virtue of a good disposition. We shall declare what the true nature of a good disposition is and that it is possible to achieve this through asceticism; we shall explain the method of this. We shall discuss the signs of a bad disposition and explain the plan for that person who recognizes his own faults. We shall discover the signs of a good disposition and explain the method for raising and training children. We shall disclose the way of the greater struggle of the disciple at the beginning of his task.

1 THE VIRTUE AND SPIRITUAL REWARD OF A GOOD DISPOSITION

Know that God Most High has praised Mustafa for his good disposition, saying: *And, lo! Thou art of a tremendous nature!* (Q. 68:4) And the Messenger said: "I was sent to complete the excellences of character." And he said: "The greatest thing placed in the scales is a good disposition."

Someone appeared before the Messenger and asked: "What is religion (*din*)?" He answered: "A good disposition." They came from the right and the left, asking (the same question again and again). He replied in the same way until at the last time he said: "Do you not know?—that you not anger." He was asked: "What is the most virtuous of actions?" He said: "A good disposition."

Someone said to the Messenger: "Give me some advice." He said: "Fear God Most High wherever you may be." (The man) said: "Another." He said: "Do a good deed after every bad act in order to erase it." (The man) said: "Another." He said: "Mix with people good-naturedly." And he said: "God Most High will not make whomever He has given a good disposition and a good appearance the food of fire."

And he was told: " Such-and-such a woman fasts by day and spends her night in formal prayer, but has a bad disposition and her tongue afflicts her neighbors." He said: "Her place is in hell." And the Messenger said: "A bad disposition ruins devotion as vinegar (ruins) honey."

And the Messenger used to say as he made supplication: "O Lord God! Thou hast created my creation well; make my disposition also good." And he used to say: "O Lord God! Grant (us) health, vigor, and a good disposition." The Messenger was asked: "What is the best thing that God Most High gives His servant?" He answered: "A good disposition." And he said: "A good disposition destroys sins as the sun (destroys) ice."

Abd al-Rahman Samurah, may God be pleased with him, says: "I was with the Messenger (🔲) He said: 'Last night I saw a strange thing: I saw a man of my own nation fallen on his knees, and there was a veil between him and God Most High. His good disposition came and lifted the veil, and he was transported to God Most High.' And he said: 'With a good disposition a person achieves the level of him who fasts by day and prays by night; he attains great degrees in the Hereafter, even though his worship is weak.'"

The best natured of people was our Messenger. One day the women were noisy and overwhelming in his presence. When Umar entered, they fled. Umar, may God be pleased with him, said (to them): "You have shame before me and have none before the Messenger of God Most High?" They said: "You are fiercer and harsher!" The Messenger said: "O son of

Khattab! By that God in Whose judgment lies my life, Satan never sees you on a road that he does not relinquish that road and travel along another out of awe for you."

Fudayl Iyad, may God have mercy upon him, said: "I prefer the company of a good-natured sinner to that of a bad-natured holy man." Ibn al-Mubarak, may God have mercy upon him, came upon a bad-natured person on the road. When he separated from him, he wept. He was asked: "Why are you weeping?" He said: "That wretch went away from me and his bad disposition went with him and did not separate from him."

Kattani, may God be pleased with him, says: "Sufism is good disposition; whoever has a better disposition than you is more of a Sufi." Yahya bin Muadh, may God be pleased with him, says: "A bad disposition is a sin which no act of devotion can benefit. A good disposition is an act of devotion to which no sin can offer harm."

(1) THE TRUE NATURE OF A GOOD DISPOSITION

Know that that much has been said about the true nature of a good disposition—as to what and which it is. Each one has talked about that (aspect) which has come before him, but not about its totality. As one says: "It is having a smiling countenance," another says: "It is taking on the troubles of other people," and another says: "It is not returning evil for evil," and so forth. All of these are its branches, but not its essence and totality. We shall disclose its true nature and the boundary of its totality.

Know that a human being has been created of two things: one is the body which can be seen with the physical eye. The other is the spirit which cannot be perceived except by the eye of the heart. For each one of these two there is goodness and unseemliness. One is called the beauty of creation; the other, the beauty of disposition. Beauty of disposition consists of the inner form, just as beauty of creation consists of the outer form. As the outer form is not good if only the eyes are good, or only the mouth is good, or only the nose is good, so that the eyes, mouth, and nose together are not good and not suited to one another; in the same way the inner form is not good so long as four powers or faculties in it are not good: the power of reason, the power of anger, the power of lust, and the power of preserving fairness and balance among the other three.

As for the power of reason, by that we mean wisdom; the goodness of which is enough to easily distinguish between truth and lies in speech, (between) the good and the unseemly in deeds, and between the true and the false in principles of belief. When this perfection has been achieved by the heart, it is from that which wisdom comes into being: the source of all kinds of happiness, as God Most High said: *And he unto whom wisdom is given, he hath truly received abundant good.* (Q. 2:269)

The goodness of the power of anger is that it be under the command of reason and the Law and arise at their command and end at their command.

The goodness of the power of the carnal appetite or lust is that it not be rebellious and that it be under the command of the Religious Law and reason so that its obedience to them may be easy for it.

The goodness of the power of justice is that it keep anger and lust subjugated to the direction of religion and reason.

The similitude of anger is that of a hunting dog; the similitude of the carnal appetite or lust is that of a horse; and the similitude of reason is that of a rider. A horse is sometimes refractory and sometimes obedient and trained. A dog is sometimes taught and sometimes it reverts to its own nature. Until the one is taught and the other trained, there is no hope for the rider's obtaining any game; indeed, there is the fear that he will be killed, that the dog may attack him, or that the horse may throw him to the ground.

The meaning of preserving justice is that both of these powers are obedient to reason and religion. Sometimes it makes lust overpower anger in order to crush (anger's) rebellion; and sometimes it makes anger overcome lust in order to crush (appetite's) greed. When all four are of this kind, a good disposition is absolute. If (only) some of them are good, this good disposition is not absolute; just like the person who has a beautiful mouth and ugly eyes, or beautiful eyes and an ugly nose: the beauty is not absolute.

Know that if each one of them is unseemly, they give birth to ugly natures and ugly deeds. The unseemliness of each power has two aspects: one is that arises from an excess which is too strong, the other from an insufficiency which is a deficit.

The power of reason, should it become excessive and involved in bad works, gives rise to deception and hypocrisy; while if it is deficient, it gives rise to foolishness and ignorance. However, when it is in balance, it gives rise to good planning, correct opinion, right thinking, and sound insight.

The power of anger, should it become excessive, is called recklessness; while if it is deficient, it is called cowardice and spiritlessness. When it is in balance—not too much or too little—it is called courage. Courage gives rise to nobility, highmindedness, bravery, mildness, patience, moderation, control of (inappropriate) anger, and characteristics like these. From recklessness come boasting, vanity, conceit, impetuosity, vainglory, throwing oneself into dangerous affairs, and the like. From its deficiency come self-abasement, helplessness, anxiety, fawning, and abjectness.

The power of lust, should it become excessive, is called gluttony. From it arise impudence, foulness, unmanliness, uncleanliness, jealousy, being despised by the powerful, being contemptuous of the poor, love of this world and the like. If it is deficient, lethargy, dastardliness, and dishonor (come).

When it is in balance, it is called temperance; from it come modesty, contentment, patience, tolerance, grace, wit, and approval.

Each one of these has two extremes which are condemned and unseemly, but the medium is good and praiseworthy. That medium, between those two extremes, is narrower than a hair. That medium is its Straight Path. It is as narrow as the Bridge of the Hereafter. Whoever walks straight upon this bridge, is sure to (cross) that (other) Bridge tomorrow (in safety).

It is for this that God Most High has ordained the middle way in all characteristics. He has forbidden both extremes, and gives punishment (for them), saying: *And those who, when they spend, are neither prodigal nor grudging; and there is a firm station between the two.* (Q. 25:67) He praised the person who does not skimp in spending and is not extravagant, but stands between the two. And the Messenger was told (by God): *And let not thy hand be chained to thy neck, nor open it with a complete opening, lest thou sit down rebuked, denuded.* (Q. 17:29) He said: "Do not tie up your hand so as to give nothing, nor open it completely at one time and give away everything lest you be left without provisions and helpless."

So then, know that the absolutely good disposition is that in which all elements are balanced and correct within it, just as a beautiful countenance is that in which all of its parts are right and good. Now, in this regard there are four types of people:

(1) One is he who achieves perfection in all of its attributes. He is the perfection of a good disposition. All creation must follow him. That is found in no one save (Muhammad) Mustafa (▢), just as Joseph (▢) was the paragon of physical beauty.

(2) The second is that all of his attributes be most unseemly. This is the absolutely bad disposition. It is a duty to expel

such a person from society, for he is close to the form of Satan, and Satan is at the extremity of unseemliness. The unseemliness of Satan is an internal unseemliness of (his) attributes and character.

(3) The third is that one is between these two degrees, but closer to goodness.

(4) The fourth is that one is the middle, but closer to unseemliness.

Just as with outward beauty where extreme goodness and extreme unseemliness are not common and most fall in between, so it is with a good disposition. Therefore, every one must make an effort so that, even if one does not achieve perfection, one comes nearer to the degree of perfection. If all of one's character is not good; well, some parts or more of it will be good. As there is not limit to the differences between beauty and ugliness, the same is true of one's character.

This is the whole meaning of a good disposition. It is not one thing, nor ten, nor a hundred; for it is much more. However, it originates with the powers of reason, anger, lust, and justice: the rest are branches of them.

(II) IT IS POSSIBLE TO ACHIEVE A GOOD DISPOSITION

Know that some have said that just as the external (appearance of) creation cannot be altered from the way it was created—short does not become tall by machination, nor does long become short, or ugly beautiful—in the same way the character which is an internal form cannot be altered. This is an error, for if that were correct training, discipline, giving advice and counsel would be useless. Did the Messenger not say: "Make your character good?" How could (alteration) be impossible when dumb animals may be trained from their stubbornness with discipline and wild prey may be domesticated? But this analogy, when applied to the disposition, is invalid because actions are of two kinds:

(1) There are some which are not affected by human choice, just as a one cannot grow an apple tree from the stone of a date; but one can grow a date palm with the nurture and care that it the requires. In the same way, the roots of anger and lust cannot be driven out of a human being. However, anger and lust can be brought to the limit of moderation with discipline. This is made plain with experience.

(2) However, with respect to some people is its more difficult. This difficulty is for two reasons: one is that it has become stronger in the essence of one's innate nature; the second is that one has been in obedience to it for a long time, to the point that one is mastered by it. In this the people are at four degrees:

(i) The first degree is that one be simple. (This person) has not yet learned good from bad and has not yet become habituated to good or bad. However, he is at the beginning of (the formation of) his nature. He can be molded and quickly corrected. He needs a person to teach him and to explain the detriment of bad character to him, and to show him the way. Children, at the beginning of their character development, are all like this. Then their fathers and mothers open the way for them and make them greedy for the world. Then they abandon them, so that they go about and live as they wish. The blood for their (loss of) religion is upon the necks of their mothers and fathers. It was for this that God Most High said: *Ward off from yourselves and your families a Fire* . . . (Q. 66:6) (ii) The second degree is that one has not yet become habituated to anything bad; however, one has made one's nature follow one's lust and anger for a time; yet, one knows that that is not to be done. His case is more difficult, for he is in need of two things: one is that he expel the corrupting nature from himself; the other is that he sow the seed of righteousness in it. However, if the earnestness and necessity appear in him, he will be corrected quickly and his nature will abstain from corruption. (iii) The third degree is that (a person's) nature has been corrupted and he does not know that that should not be done, for (corruption) appears good to him. He will not be amenable to correction, except rarely. (iv) The fourth degree it that, with all of this, (a person) glories in his corruption and supposes that it is some skill, as the braggarts who say: "We have killed so many people," or: "We have drunk so much wine." This person is incurable, unless some heavenly happiness reach him which does not carry him on the path.

(III) THE MANNER OF TREATMENT

Know that for whoever desires to expel his bad disposition from himself there is only one way, and that is that he do the opposite of whatever that (bad) disposition commands him (to do). Lust or carnal appetite cannot be broken except by opposition. Everything is overcome by its contrary, just as the treatment of an illness which causes heat is the eating of cold (foods). The treatment of every illness which arises from anger is patience. The treatment of whatever arises from arrogance is humility. The treatment of whatever arises from miserliness is giving away wealth. The same (rule) is valid for all.

Consequently, a good disposition appears in anyone who has made a habit of good works. The inmost mystery of the Religious Law's commanding good works is that its purpose is the transformation of the heart from an unseemly form to a good form. Whatever habit a person does by compulsion becomes his nature. At the beginning, a child tries to escape from school and teaching, but when he is forced to study, it becomes his habit. When he grows up, all of his pleasure is in knowledge. He cannot keep himself away from it. Indeed, a person who has become habituated to gaming with pigeons, playing chess, or gambling, so that it becomes second-nature to him, will give all the comforts of the world and all that he has for those (pursuits) and cannot keep away from them. Things which are contrary to one's temperament become of the temperament by reason of habit.

There are people who take pride—out of being roving charlatans—in enduring being beaten with clubs and having their hands cut off. (There are) effeminates who, despite the despicableness of their deeds, glory in their effeminacy. Indeed, if one looks among cuppers and sweepers, they too boast about their own work to each other among themselves, as do the learned and kings together. All these are the fruits of habit. Moreover, there is the person who has become accustomed to eating clay, and is become so that he cannot keep away from it and continues to endure illness and the danger of death (from it).

Therefore, since that which is contrary to nature becomes natural by habit, it is better that that which is consonant with one's nature and is for the heart as food and drink is for the body be obtained through worship, the knowledge of God Most High, and devotion to Him. Keeping anger and lust under control is appropriate to human nature, for (that nature) is of the essence of the angels and (doing that) is his nourishment. He whose inclination is contrary to this has become sick so that his nourishment has become unpleasant to him. As for the sick person, it may be he holds the nourishment in enmity while he becomes eager for that which is harmful to him.

Consequently, anyone who likes something more than the knowledge of God Most High and obedience to (Him) is sick. As God Most High said: *There is a sickness in their hearts.* (Q. 2:10) And He said: *Except him who comes to God with a sound heart.* (Q. 26:89) As the sick body is in danger of ruin in this world, so the sick heart is in danger of ruin in the next world. As there is no hope of recovery for the sick person except that which is contrary to his own desires, he takes bitter medicine at the doctor's order; so, too, for the sick heart there is no stratagem except opposition to the appetites of the self at the word of the Master of the Religious Law, peace be upon him, who is the physician of the people's hearts.

To summarize, physical medicine and spiritual medicine both have one method: the cooling of the hot, and the heating of the cold. In the same way, a person who is dominated by pride is cured by being compelled to be humble; and if a person is dominated by humility reaching the point of meanness, he is cured by being compelled to be (more) prideful. Now, know that there are three reasons for good character:

(i) One is that it is innate: it is a gift and a favor from God Most High for a person to be created with an innate good disposition. For example, one is created generous, another is created humble, and there are many like that. (ii) The second is that one can force oneself to become accustomed to doing good works so that it becomes habitual. (iii) The third is that one sees persons whose character and deeds are good. One should associate with them so as to necessarily take upon himself those attributes, even if he is not aware of (the transformation).

He in whom these three felicities appear—having an innate good character, having association with the good, and making good works a habit—is at the degree of perfection. Whoever is deprived of these three things—one whose innate character is deficient, one who associates with scoundrels, and who makes a habit of evil deeds—is at the degree of perfect wretchedness.

Between these (two extremes) there are many degrees, having more or less, and the happiness and wretchedness for each is according to their amounts. (On that day people will come forth in sundry bodies that they may be shown their works.) *So he who does an atom's weight of good will see it. And he who does an atom's weight of evil will see it.* (Q. 99:6-8)

(IV) [THE BEGINNING OF ALL (SPIRITUAL) HAPPINESS IS TAKING PAINS IN (DOING) GOOD DEEDS]

Know that actions are (the province) of the limbs of the body, but the objective (of actions) is the turning round of the heart; for it is the heart that will travel to the next world. Everything must be beautiful and perfect so as to be appropriate to the Divine Presence. It must be straight like an untarnished mirror so as to reflect the Heavenly Form in it and to see a Beauty that will beggar the descriptions of heaven that one has heard. Even though the body will also have a portion in that world, the heart is primary and the body secondary.

Know that the heart is one thing and the body another. The heart is of the celestial world and the body of the visible world. . . . [1]

However, even though the body is separate from the heart, nonetheless it has a connection with it; for from each good act of the body a light attaches itself to the heart, while for from every bad act of the body a darkness attaches itself to the heart. That light is the seed of (spiritual) happiness and that darkness is the seed of (spiritual) misery. It is because of this connection that a person is brought to this world: in order that he make of his body a net and an instrument to acquire the attributes of perfection for himself.

Know that writing is an art which is an attribute of the heart, but its action is by the fingers. If a person desires that his handwriting be good, the method is that he continually write in a good hand so that the form of the writing becomes beautiful. When that is accomplished, the fingers begin to receive that shape from inside and to put it into the writing. So in the same manner, from the external good act one's inner self begins to assume a good character. When good character has become an internalized attribute, then deeds assume the attributes of that character.

Therefore, the beginning of all (spiritual) happiness is taking pains in (the performance of) good deeds. The fruit of this is that the heart internalizes good qualities; then their light shines outside and good deeds begin to be accepted naturally and voluntarily. The mystery of this is that connection which is between the heart and the body, for one affects the other and vice versa. It is for this that any act done negligently is in vain, because the heart has not given that act any part of its attributes because the heart was unaware of it.

(V) [ALL GOOD CHARACTER MUST BECOME NATURAL]

Know that the sick person whose illness is coldness should not eat things which are very hot, for it may be that the heat become an illness. Rather, there is a scale and a standard which must be observed. It must be known that the objective is that the temperament be equable: neither inclining to heat, nor inclining to cold. When it has reached the level of equability, the treatment is withdrawn and the effort becomes the maintenance of that balance. (The patient) eats temperate things.

In the same manner, all character has two aspects: one is praiseworthy and one is blameworthy. The objective is moderation. For example, we order the miser to give away wealth until it becomes easy for him, but not to the point of extravagance; for that is also blameworthy. But the scale for (weighing) that is from the Religious Law, just as the scale for (weighing) the treatment of the body is the science of medicine. He must become so that whatever the Law commands him to give, he gives, and its giving becomes easy for him and that there not be in him a demand to keep and hold on to (wealth). And whatever the Religious Law commands him to keep, he should keep and the urge to give (of that) not be in him so that he be moderate. Therefore, if those impulses continue to appear in him—but he represses them by force—he is still ill; however, he is praiseworthy because he is indeed forcing himself to take his medicine and this compulsion is the way that (good character) will become natural to him.

It is for this that the Messenger said: "Obey the command of God Most High; if you cannot, then (obey Him) with displeasure, for there is much goodness in being patient." Know that every person who forces himself to give away wealth is not generous; rather, generous is the person for whom giving away wealth is easy. Whoever forces himself to retain wealth is not a miser; rather, the miser is the person whose nature it is to keep (things).

Therefore, all character should be natural and taking pains should depart. Indeed, the perfection of character is that one surrenders one's reins to the hand of the Religious Law and that obedience to it becomes easy. No struggle remains (against it) in one. As God Most High said: *But no, by thy Lord! They believe not until they make thee (oh Muhammad) a judge of what is in dispute between them, then find not any straitness in their hearts* . . . (Q. 4:65) He said: "Their faith will be completed by making you their judge, not retaining any heaviness or narrowness in their hearts." There is a mystery for this to which a reference has been made even though this book could not contain (the mystery itself).

Know that the (spiritual) happiness of a human being is that one becomes of the nature of angels; for one's essence is of them and one has come into this world a stranger. One's source is the world of the angels. Every foreign characteristic that one bears from here distances one from being in conformity with (the angels). When going to that place, one must become of their character and not carry any attributes from this place.

Whoever is avid for the preservation of wealth is obsessed

with wealth; and whoever is avid to spend it is also obsessed with wealth. Whoever is intent upon being haughty is obsessed with people; and whoever is intent upon being humble is also obsessed with people. But the angels are neither obsessed with wealth nor with people; indeed, because of their love for the Divine Presence they pay attention to nothing else.

Therefore, the connection of the human being to wealth must be severed and cut off from people so that (the spiritual heart) may be cleansed of all of them. Any attribute which it is not possible for a person to eliminate, should be kept at the (the level of) moderation so that in one way it is as though it were eliminated. As water is not devoid of warmth or coldness, that which is tepid and equable resembles that which is devoid of both (extremes). Therefore, moderation and the mean in all qualities have been commanded because they are better.

So, the heart should be observed as to whether it is cut off from all and immersed in God Most High. As He said: *Say: I ask you not for any reward for (the Quran). It is naught but a Reminder to the nations.* (Q. 6:91) Indeed, the reality of "there is no god but God" is exactly this. Because it is not possible for a human being to be free of all contamination, He said: *And there is not one of you but shall come to it. This is an unavoidable decree of thy Lord.* (Q. 19:71)

Finally, from this it is plain that end of all disciplines and the aim of all exertions is that a person reach the Unity of God: that he see it and naught else, that he read it and naught else, that he be obedient to it and naught else. In his inner being no other urge remains. When it is thus, a good character has been achieved. Indeed, one has passed over from the world of mankind and reached the true nature of God.

(VI) [THE WAYS OF ACHIEVING A GOOD CHARACTER]

Know that ascetic self-discipline is a difficult and torturous task, but if the physician is a master and knows pleasant medicine for the way, it becomes much easier. It is the physician's grace that he does not call the disciple at first to the degree of the true nature of God, for he would not have the strength to endure that. If one says to a child: "Go to the school until you reach the level of principalship." (The child) does not know what the pleasure of principalship may be. Instead, one should say: "Go to the school and I shall give you a stick and a ball tonight to play with," so that the child will go to school out of a desire for that. When he gets older, one persuades him with fine clothing and ornaments so that he will refrain from play. When he gets older, one promises him with mastership and chieftainship and says: "Silk clothing is for women." When he is older, then one says: "Mastership and chieftainship of the world have no basis, for death will destroy all of them." Then one promises him the everlasting kingdom.

Consequently, it may be that the student at the beginning of the task not be able to be completely sincere. One is patient with him so that he continue to strive in the eagerness that people will look upon him favorably, until one shatters the inclination to wilful deception, the greed of the belly, and the greed for wealth in him. When he has been liberated from those, a sluggishness appears in him. Then one must dispel the greed for that sluggishness in him by commanding him to beg in the marketplace. When an acceptance of that appears in him, one should prevent that by engaging him in some menial tasks, such as cleaning lavatories, etc.

In the same way, one must gradually order the treatment for each characteristic that appears in him; (but) not all at once, for he would not be able to endure that. There are many kinds of harms resulting from wilful deception. For example, all such characteristics are like serpents and scorpions. The similitude of wilful deception is the dragon which swallows everything. The last of the characteristics to depart from the truly righteous is that.

2 RECOGNIZING THE SICKNESS OF THE HEART

Know that just as the soundness of the body, hands, feet, and eyes lies in that each one of them is able to do completely that for which it was created—so that the eye sees well and the foot walks well—so the soundness of the heart lies in that its special quality that is part of its original innate nature and the reason for which it was created. It is to be the loving friend of that which is basis of original innate nature and this should be easy for the heart.

(i) *[THE SIGNS OF A HEART'S SOUNDNESS]*

This is found in two things: one in will and the other in power.

(1) As for the will: in it there is nothing more preferred than God Most High, for the gnosis (*marifat*) of God Most High is the nourishment of the heart, just as food is the nourishment of the body. A body from which the craving for food has departed or in which it has grown weak is sick. A heart from which the love for God Most High has departed or in which it has grown weak is sick. It is for this that God Most High said: *Say: If your fathers and your sons. . .* (Q. 9:24) "If you love your fathers, your sons, your wives, your kinsfolk, and that which you possess more than God Most High be patient until the command of God Most High arrives and you shall see!"

(2) As for the power, it is that obedience to God Most High has become easy and one finds no need to coerce oneself in that. Rather, it is in itself one's pleasure. As the Messenger said: "Formal prayer has become the light of my eyes."

Therefore, for a person who does not find these two qualities in himself, this is a certain symptom of his heart's sickness: he must attend to its treatment. It may be that he think
that (his spiritual heart) is of that character, while it is not; for
a person is (often) blind to his own faults.

(II) THE DEFECTS OF THE HEART

The defects of the heart can be recognized in four ways:

(1) One is that one resort to an experienced and mature
spiritual guide so that that spiritual guide may examine him
and disclose the person's defects to him. In this era, this is
unusual and rare.

(2) The second is that one have a sympathetic friend watch
over oneself, one who will not conceal one's defects out of flat-
tery nor magnify them out of envy. This too is rare. Dawud
Tayi, may God have mercy upon him, was asked: "Why do you
not associate and mix with people?" He replied: "What is the
point of associating with a people who see my faults and conceal them from me?"

(3) The third is that one listen to the talk of one's enemies
about oneself, for the eye of the enemy always falls upon
faults. Even if he exaggerates out of his enmity, his words are
still not devoid of truth.

(4) The fourth is that one should study people. One should
constantly be on the watch for any defect in oneself that one
sees in someone else. One should suspect one's self, for it may
be the same.

Jesus (☐) was asked: "Who taught you the rules of conduct?" He replied: "No one. I kept away from whatever I found
unseemly in others." Know that the more foolish a person is,
the more he considers himself good. The more intelligent one
is, the more he suspects himself. Umar, may God be pleased
with him, used to ask Hudhayfah, may God be pleased with

him: "The Messenger has told you the secret of the hypocrites. What signs of hypocrisy do you find in me?" So, each person must seek out his own faults, for it he does not know the disease, he cannot remedy it.

All remedies meet the opposition of the lust or carnal appetite; as God Most High said: *But as for him who feared to stand before his Lord and restrained his soul from lust, lo! Paradise shall be his home.* (Q. 79:40-41)

The Messenger used to say to the Companions when they returned from battle in defense of religion: "Ye have come from the lesser struggle to the greater struggle." They asked: "What is that?" He answered: "The striving against one's animal soul (*jihad-i nafs*)." And the Messenger said: "Restrain the torment of yourself from the animal soul and do give rein to its whims in disobedience to God Most High Who will judge you tomorrow and curse you until your parts all curse one another."

Hasan Basri, may God be pleased with him, says: "There is no headstrong steed more difficult to rein in that the animal soul." Sari Saqti, may God have mercy upon him, says: "For forty years my animal soul has wished me to dip a round cake into honey and eat it, but I have not yet done so."

Ibrahim Khawwas, may God have mercy upon him, says: "I was walking on Mount Lukkam in Lebanon and I saw a lot of pomegranates. I felt a desire for some. I picked one; it was sour. I withheld my hand and went on my way. I saw a fallen man. Bees were collecting around him and stinging him. He said: 'Peace be upon you, Ibrahim.' I asked: 'How did you know who I was?' He said: 'Nothing is concealed from whoever knows God Most High.' I said: 'I see that you have some state with God Most High. Why do you not ask Him to keep the bees away from you?' He said: 'You too have a state. Why do you not ask that He take away the craving for pomegranates, for the wounds of the appetites are in the next world, and the wounds of the bees are in this world.'"

7

Know that even though the pomegranate is lawful, yet the prudent have learned that the appetite for both the lawful and the unlawful is the same. If you do not shut the door of the lawful upon (the appetite) and you do not return it to the limit of only what is necessary, it will seek the unlawful. For this reason, they have forbidden the appetites to themselves with respect to permitted things in order to escape appetite. As Umar, may God be pleased with him, said: "I have refrained from seventy categories of lawful things out fear that I may fall into the unlawful."

Another reason is that when the animal soul becomes accustomed to comfort and ease, it acquires a love for the permitted things of the world and the heart becomes attached to them, turning this world into its heaven. Death becomes difficult. Rudeness and heedlessness appear in one's heart. When he engages in the remembrance (of God) and intimate conversation (with God), he finds no pleasure in it. Not craving lawful desires makes him turn to (love of remembering of God). He becomes discomfited and troubled. The world becomes hateful to him and an eagerness for the comfort of the Hereafter appears in his heart. In a state of sorrow and broken-heartedness, a single glorification will have the effect upon his heart that hundreds (of glorifications) did not have when he was in a state of joy and ease.

The similitude of the animal soul is the falcon that is trained by putting it into a chamber and covering its eyes so as to restrain from all that was in it of its falcon-ness. Then, gradually, it will be given meat so that it may become familiar with the falconer and obedient to him. In the same way, the heart does not find intimacy with God Most High so long as you do not wean it from all habits and do not close off the eyes, tongue, and eyes (to such things), and you do not discipline it with seclusion, hunger, silence, and sleeplessness. In the beginning this will be difficult for it—just as when a child is

weaned from milk. Afterwards, (the child) will becomes so that
if one tries to give him milk by force, he will not be able to
drink it.

Know that the spiritual discipline for every person is that
he give up whatever it is that pleases him more and that he do
the contrary of whatever (tendency) is more dominant. The
person whose delight is rank and pomp must abandon them.
The one whose happiness is wealth must spend it. In the same
way, one must forcibly sever oneself from any source of happiness other than God Most High. One must attend upon that
which will attend upon one forever. One should abandon voluntarily all that one will abandon at death. One's attendant is
God Most High, as God Most High revealed to David (D): "O
David, I am thy Attendant; be thou My attendant." And the
Messenger said: "Gabriel breathed into me (the words): Love
whom you will; verily thou wilt be separated from him." Love
whomever you will of the world, for he will be taken from you.
Peace!

3 THE SIGNS OF A GOOD CHARACTER

Know that the signs of a good character are those which
God Most High has described concerning the believers in the
Quran in the first ten verses of the chapter beginning:
Successful indeed are the believers, (Q. 23:1-10) and in the
verse where He says: *Those who turn in repentance and those
who serve (Him) . . .*, (Q. 9:112) and in those verses where He
says: *And the servants of the Compassionate are they who walk
upon the earth modestly to the end* (of the chapter). (Q. 25:63-
77)

And whatever He has said about the signs of the hypocrites are the signs of a bad character. As the Messenger said:
"The aspiration of the believer is formal prayer, fasting, and
worship, but the aspiration of the hypocrite is food and drink,
like that of a dumb animal." Hatim Asamm, may God have

mercy upon him, says: "The believer is occupied with reflection and admonition while the hypocrite is occupied with envy and expectation. The believer is safe from everyone save God Most High while the hypocrite fears everyone save God Most High. The believer has no hope from anyone save God Most High while the hypocrite has hopes from everyone save God Most High. The believer sacrifices his wealth for religion while the hypocrite sacrifices his religion for wealth. The believer is always obedient and always weeping while the hypocrite is always sinning and always laughing. The believer prefers solitude and seclusion while the hypocrite prefers mixing and crowds. The believer always sows and fears that he not will not reap while the hypocrite never sows and is ambitious to reap."

And it has been said thus: "A person of good character is he who is modest, says little, causes little trouble, speaks the truth, seeks the good, worships much, has few faults, meddles little, desires the good for all, and does good works for all. He is compassionate, dignified, measured, patient, content, grateful, sympathetic, friendly, abstinent, and not greedy. He does not use foul language, nor does he exhibit haste, nor does he harbor hatred in his heart. He is not envious. He is candid, well-spoken, and his friendship and enmity, his anger and his pleasure are for the sake of God Most High and nothing more."

Know that good character usually comes from endurance and patience, just as when the Messenger was much tormented and his teeth were broken, he said: "O Lord God! Show them the way for they do not know."

Ibrahim Adham, may God have mercy upon him, was crossing a plain. A soldier came to him and asked: "Are you a captive?" He answered: "Yes." (The soldier) asked: "Where is there a town?" (Ibrahim) pointed to a cemetery. (The soldier) said: "I am looking for a settlement." (Ibrahim) said: "It is a settlement there." The soldier struck him with a club so hard

that (Ibrahim) was covered with blood. The soldier grabbed
him and dragged him to the city. When (Ibrahim's) friends saw
him, they cried to the soldier: "Fool! This is Ibrahim Adham,
the nonpareil of this epoch!" The soldier dismounted from his
horse and kissed (Ibrahim's) feet. Then he asked him: "Why
did you say you were a captive?" Ibrahim answered: "Because
I am a slave of God Most High." (The soldier) asked: "Why did
you indicate the cemetery as a settlement?" He said: "There is
a promise for all there; therefore it is a settlement." The soldier said: "As I have behaved rudely, forgive me." Then
Ibrahim said: "When he broke my head, I offered supplications
for him." They asked: "Why?" He answered: "Because I knew
that there would be spiritual reward for me because of him. I
did not desire that my portion be better than his and his portion be worse than mine."

Abu Uthman Hiri was invited by someone to test him.
When he arrived at the door of the house, (the host) did not
allow him to enter, saying: "There is nothing left." (Abu
Uthman) went back. After he had gone a short distance, (the
host) came after him and called him to come back. (Abu
Uthman) returned. When he arrived at the door of the house,
(the host) would not admit him and said the same thing. (Abu
Uthman) left. (The host) did this several times: his calling
(Abu Uthman), (Abu Uthman's) arriving and then being
turned away and his departure. (The host) said: "What a good
character you have!" (Abu Uthman) said: "That which you
have seen of me is the character of a dog. When you call him,
he comes; when you drive him away, he goes. How valuable is
that?"

One day someone emptied a basin of ashes from a roof on
(Abu Uthman Hiri's) head. He wiped off his clothing and gave
thanks. He was asked: "Why did you give thanks?" He said: "It
is a cause for thanks when they make peace with a person who
deserves Fire with ashes."

Ali bin Musa al-Rida, may God have mercy upon him, had
a swarthy color. There was a bathhouse by the door of his res-
idence in Nishabur. When he used to go the bathhouse they
would empty it. One day they emptied the bathhouse and he
went into it. The bathhousekeeper was inattentive. A villager
entered the bath. Seeing (Ali bin Musa), he thought that he
was a servant of the bath. (The villager) said: "Get up! Bring
water!" (Ali bin Musa) brought some water. Then (the villager)
said: "Get up and bring some clay." He brought some. (The villager) continued to issue orders and (Ali bin Musa) continued
to execute them. When the bathhousekeeper returned and
heard the villager addressing (Ali bin Musa), he grew afraid
and fled. When (Ali bin Musa) came out of the bath he was
told that the bathhousekeeper had fled out of fear because of
the incident. (Ali bin Musa) said: "Tell him not to flee. The
offense was not his."

Abd Allah the Tailor (Darzi), may God have mercy upon
him, was of the great ones of his age. A Magian used to order
garments from him every year and pay him each time with
adulterated silver. He would accept it and say nothing. One
time he was absent and his apprentice refused to accept the
adulterated silver coins. When (Abd Allah) came back, he
asked: "Why did you do that? He has been doing that to me for
many years and I have not tasked him with it. I accepted (the
false money) so that (another) Muslim would not be deceived
by that bad money and so that I could bury it."

Uways Qarani, may God be pleased with him, used to go
walking and some children would throw stones at him. He
would say: "Indeed! Throw small stones lest my legs be broken
and I not be able to stand to perform formal prayer." Someone
used to insult Ahnaf Qays, may God be pleased with him.
(That person) would go along with him and (Ahnaf) would
remain silent. When he approached his own tribe he stood and
said to that person: "If you have anything more to say, say it

here; for if my people hear you, they will injure you." A woman said to Malik Dinar: "O hypocrite!" He replied: "The people of Basrah had lost my name; you have found it again!"

These are the signs of the perfection of good character which those people had. They are the qualities of persons who, by self-discipline, have totally cleansed themselves of the qualities of (their) human nature and see nothing except God Most High. Whatever they see, they see as from Him. A person who, because of his animal soul, does not see this, nor any little thing resembling it, must not deceive himself and suppose himself to have a good character. Peace!

4 THE RAISING AND TRAINING OF CHILDREN

Know that a child is a trust in the hands of the mother and father. His pure heart is a precious gem that can be molded like wax and it is a *tabula rasa*. It is like clean earth which will grow any seed you throw into it. If you a sow good seed, it will achieve the happiness of religion and the world, and the mother, father, and teacher will share in the spiritual reward of that. If it is its the opposite, then (the child) will be miserable and they will share in whatever (misfortune) comes to him. God Most High says: *Ward off from yourselves and your families a Fire.* (Q. 66:6) Preserve yourselves and your children from the fire of hell. It is more important to protect your children from the fire of hell than from the fire of this world.

Protecting him is by means of training him, instilling a good character in him, and protecting him from bad companions; for the origins of all kinds of corruption arise from bad companions. He should not be habituated to comfort and ease and to wearing fine clothing, for then he will not be able to do without them and will waste his entire life in trying to get them. Rather, one should try from the very beginning, so that the woman whose milk he drinks should be righteous, of good

character, and one whose subsistence is lawful, because a bad
character spreads from the wet nurse, and the milk which is
produced from unlawful nourishment is unclean. The flesh
and skin of the child develops from (that unlawful milk) and
an affinity to that (unlawfulness) will develop in his nature
that will become apparent after puberty.

When (the child) begins to talk, his first word must be
"God" (Allah), and this must be continually prompted to him.
When he begins to feel shame about some things, this is good
news and the proof that the enlightening rays of reason have
fallen upon him. He makes a policeman out of shame that
embarrasses him at every unseemliness.

The first thing that will be discovered in (the infant) is a
voracious appetite for nourishment. One must begin teaching
him the behavior of eating so that he eats with the right hand,
saying: "In the name of God" (*bismillah*). (He should) not eat
rapidly, and chew small bites; nor should he look at what others are eating, nor take another morsel in his hand until he
has swallowed that one in his mouth. (He should) not soil his
hand and clothing. From time to time give him plain bread so
that he not become habituated to stew. One should make over-
eating appear unseemly to him and say: "That is the way of
dumb animals and the unwise." One should criticize a child
who eats too much in his presence and praise a child who eats
little and observes the rules of etiquette in his presence, so
that the vein of pride may pulse in him and he too become like
that.

One should make white clothing seem good to his eye, and
one should hold silken and colored clothing blameworthy to
his eye, saying: "Those are the affair of women and lovelies,
and self-adornment is the affair of the effeminate, not the
affair of men." One should take care that children wearing silk
garments and enjoying comfort and ease do not fall in with

him and that he does not see them; for that will be his ruin as he will also desire them. One should keep (the child) from bad companions. Every child not so guarded will become impudent, lying, stubborn, and reckless. These (qualities) will not depart from his nature for long time.

When he is handed over to school, he learns the Quran. After that, he studies the Traditions, the stories of the saints, the lives of the Companions and the forefathers. Of course one does not permit him to occupy himself with verses in which there is talk of love and the characteristics of women. One should guard him from the teacher who says: "One's nature becomes refined with that." He is not a teacher; rather, he is a devil who is sowing the seed of corruption in (the child).

When the child is working well and a good character appears in him, he should be praised and one should give him something to make him happy, and one should praise him before others. However, if he makes a mistake once or twice, it should be overlooked so that words (of admonition) not become ineffectual, especially if (the error) is not public. If one talks too much to him, he will become emboldened and commit (the mistake) openly. When he continues to repeat (the mistake), one should reprimand him privately, saying: "Take care that no one learn this about you, for you will be disgraced among the people and you will be held of account." The father should keep his dignity with him and the mother make him fear his father.

One should not permit him to sleep during the day; he will become lazy. He should not sleep upon soft bedclothes at night so that his body will grow strong. One should not prevent him for playing an hour everyday so that he will become well trained and not become gloomy, which leads to a bad nature and his becoming dull. One should make him accustomed to being humble with all persons and to refrain from boasting or bragging to other children.

He should not accept anything from (other) children; rather, he should give to them. He should be told: "Accepting (things) is the work of beggars and those lacking in good ambition." He should, of course, not open himself to the appetite for gold, silver, and goods that he receives from another person, for he will be spoiled by that and fall into unbecoming habits.

One should teach him that he should not to spit or blow the fluid out of his nose in the presence of others. He should not turn his back upon people; he should sit properly and not put his hand under his chin, for that is the proof of indolence. He should not talk much and, of course, not swear oaths. He should not speak until addressed. He should respect those older than he, and he should not approach them (on his own). He should eschew curses and foul language. If the teacher beats him, one should tell him not to cry out, complain too much, or rouse an intercessor. He should be patient and say: "This is the work of men. Crying aloud is the work of women and serving girls."

When he is seven years old, he should be ordered to perform the formal prayers and observe the rules of purification. When he is ten years old, if he misses formal prayer, one should beat and correct him. One should make theft, eating the unlawful, and lying unseemly in his eyes and always treat them with contempt.

When he is brought up like this, he is told the underlying reasons for these rules of conduct when he achieves puberty: "The object of food is that it give strength to the servant for devotion to God Most High. The purpose of the world is the acquisition of the provisions for Hereafter—for the world does not remain with a person and death comes unexpectedly—so that one may achieve Paradise and the pleasure of God Most High. One begins to describe heaven and hell and the spiritual reward or punishment for deeds to him. If he has been reared with good training from the beginning, these words will be as though engraved upon stone (for him). If he has been left on his own, (these words) will fall to the ground like dust from a wall.

Sahl Tustari, may God have mercy upon him, says: "I was three years old when I used to watch my maternal uncle, Muhammad (bin) Suwar, when he performed the evening obligatory formal prayer. One time he said to me: 'Do you not remember that God who created you at all, lad?' I said: 'How do I do that?' He said: 'When you get into your bedding at night, say three times—in your heart, not aloud—"God Most High is with me. God Most High is watching me. God Most High sees me."' I said: 'I have been saying that for a number of nights.' Then he said: 'Say it seven times every night.' I did that; then he said: 'Say it fifteen times every night.' I did that and then the sweetness of that fell into my heart. After a year, he said to me: 'Remember what I have told you all your life, until that time when they place you in your grave. It will hold your hand in this world and the next.' I continued to repeat (his words) for a number of years until their sweetness appeared in my conscience. Then one day, my uncle said to me: 'Whomever God is with and whomever He observes and whomever He sees does not sin. Take care that you do not sin, for He sees you.'

"Then I was sent to a school. I was upset. I said: 'Do not send (there) for more than an hour every day.' That was until I had learned the Quran; I was seven years old. When I was ten, I continually fasted and ate barley bread until I was twelve. In my thirteenth year, a question entered my mind. I said: 'Send me to Basrah so that I may ask the religious scholars of Basrah.' I was sent there. I asked all of the religious scholars, but they could not resolve it. I went to Abbadan where a man had been suggested to me. He resolved my problem. I stayed with him for a while, then I came to Tustar and I bought some barley with a silver dirham, breaking my fast with barley bread without any stew or sauce. I made do with that silver dirham for a year. Then I decided to go three days and nights without eating anything in order to inure myself to that. Then I did it for a five-day period, then seven days, until I was able to fast for twenty-five days and nights without eating anything. I endured this for twenty years and remained awake at night (in prayer and supplication)."

This story has been related to that is may become plain that the seed for every great deed is sown in childhood. Peace!

5 THE PREREQUISITES OF THE DISCIPLE

Know that the reason for someone's not reaching God is that he has not traveled the path. The reason for someone's not traveling the path is that he has not sought it. The reason for someone's not seeking it is the he did not know, and his belief was incomplete. Indeed, the desire for the quest for the provisions of the Hereafter appears in whoever knows that the world causes misery and is but of a few days in duration, while the Hereafter is pure and everlasting. It is not a hardship for him to exchange something despicable for something valuable. Putting down the earthen jug so that tomorrow one will receive a golden jug is not very difficult.

Therefore, the cause of all of this is the weakness of faith, and the cause of the weakness of faith is the disappearance of guides who lead and guide the way of the abstemious religious scholar. None of these are left. As there are no leaders and guides, the way remains empty and people have been deprived of their (spiritual) happiness. Those who are left of the religious scholars, their hearts have been overcome by the love of the world. Since they are in search of the world, how can they summon the people from the world to the Hereafter? The way of the world is opposite to the way of the Hereafter The world and the Hereafter are like the East and the West; to whichever you draw closer, you go farther away from the other.

Consequently, if the desire for God Most High appears in someone, and he is one of those about whom God Most High says: *And he who desires the Hereafter...* (Q. 17:19) He should know what the effort and striving is required. God continues: *... and strives for it with the effort necessary.* (Q. 17:19) Know that this effort is traveling the way! The traveler must first possess certain requisites which he has previously accomplished; then there is the document that he must hold firmly; then there is a fortress and a castle which will give him refuge.

(I) [THE VEILS BETWEEN GOD AND THE CREATED]

It is a condition that one first lift the veil between the self and God so as not to be one of those people about whom God Most High says: *We have set a barrier before them and a barrier behind them (and have covered them so that they see not)* (Q. 36.9) The veils are four: wealth, rank or status, following precedent, (imitation) and sin.

As for wealth, it is a veil when it engages the heart. The way cannot be traveled except with an unencumbered heart. Wealth must be removed except for that necessary amount which will not preoccupy (one). If there is someone who has nothing and another takes care of him, his way will be completed more quickly.

As for the veil of rank and pomp, one must arise and flee from them. One must go to some place where one is not known. If one is well known, one will always be engaged with people and with the pleasure of their reception (of him). Whosoever's pleasure is derived from people will not reach God.

As for following precedent or imitation, it is a veil because if one believes in someone's school of Religious Law and hears its words in the way of argument, one gives no place to anything else in his heart. One forgets that one should believe in the significance of "there is no god but God" and that one should seek the fulfillment of that in oneself. The fulfillment of that is that one has no object of worship which he obeys except God Most High. Whoever is overcome by passion (animal soul), that passion is one's object of worship. When this state becomes (one's) true nature, one must uncover or discover it through greater struggle, not through argument.

As for sin, it is the greatest veil. The heart of whoever perseveres in sin is dark. How can God be revealed to him? Especially (the consumption of) forbidden food, for it annihilates the effect lawful food makes in illuminating the heart. In reality, one must beware of the forbidden morsel and consume only lawful food. Anyone who wishes that the mysteries of religion and the Religious Law be unveiled to him before he observes and implements the externals of the Religious Law in dealings is like the person who wishes to read the Arabic commentaries on the Quran before he has learned Arabic.

(II) [THE GUIDE OF THE WAY]

When these veils have been pulled away, (the person's) similitude is that of the person who has performed the obligatory purification and is prepared to perform the (obligatory) formal prayer. Now he needs an imam to lead him (in performing the prayer). That is spiritual guide, for without a spiritual guide traveling the path will not be direct. The path to God is hidden and mixed with the paths of Satan. The path to God is one, but there are a thousand paths to the false. How will it be possible to travel that (one) path without a guide? When one has found his spiritual guide, he must put all of his affairs in (the guide's) hands and set aside control over himself. He must know that his profit in the spiritual guide's error will be greater than in his own correctness. Whatever he hears from the spiritual guide that he does not understand should remind him of the story of Moses and Khidr, peace be upon them both. That story is for the spiritual guide and his disciple, for the shaykhs know things which the mind (of the disciple) cannot entertain.

In the time of Galen someone developed a pain in a finger of his right hand. Physicians of insufficient knowledge applied medicine to that finger, but there was no improvement. Galen applied some medicine to (the man's) left shoulder. They said: "What kind of nonsense is this? The pain is here and the medicine is there! What use is that?" The finger got better. The reason was that (Galen) knew that the defect had occurred in the main nerve, and he knew that nerves spring from the brain and the spine, and that which comes from the left goes to the right, and that which comes from the right goes to the left. The point of this example is that it be known that no control must remain within the disciple.

I heard about Khwajah Abu Ali Farmudhi, may God have mercy upon him, that he said: "Once I was recounting a dream to my shaykh, Abu al-Qasim Gurgani, may God have mercy upon him, who was my spiritual guide. He grew angry and did not speak to me for a month. I did not know any cause for that until the time he said: 'During the telling of the story of the dream you said: "You, who are a shaykh, spoke to me thus in a dream. (In the dream) I asked you: 'Why?'"' He said: 'If inside you there had been no room for "Why?" you would not have uttered it in a dream.'"

Therefore, when the affair is entrusted to the spiritual guide, the first act of the spiritual guide is to place him in a fortress so that evils not circle around him. That fortress has four walls: one is seclusion, another is silence, another is hunger, and another is wakefulness. Hunger closes the way of Satan, sleeping little illuminates the heart, silence keeps the heart from the distraction of talk, and seclusion turns away the darkness of people from him and closes the way to the eyes and ears. Sahl Tustari, may God have mercy upon him, says: "The saints who have become saints became so by seclusion, hunger, silence, and wakefulness."

When one has arisen out of the path of preoccupation (with this world), one starts to travel on the path. The beginning of the path is that one starts to overcome the first obstacles of the path. The obstacles of the path are the blameworthy qualities in the heart. They are the root of the things from which one must flee—such as the greed for wealth and rank, the greed for comfort, haughtiness, hypocrisy, and the like—until the materials of distraction are cut off from within and the heart is empty (of them). It may happen that a person be emptied of all of these until he is not polluted by more than one (blameworthy quality). Then he must strive to sever that one by the means which the shaykh approves and considers more suited (to him), for these vary with conditions.

Now that he has cleared the field, the sowing of seed begins. The seed is the remembrance of God Most High, since he has been emptied of all save Him. Then he sits in seclusion and continually recites *al-Lah, al-Lah* in his heart and with his tongue until the time when the tongue falls silent and the heart begins to speak. Then the heart, too, ceases to speak and the spirit and meaning of the word overwhelms the heart; the significance is not in the letters. It is not Arabic or Persian, for speaking with the heart is also speech. Speech is the sheathe and the husk of the seed, not the seed itself. Then, the import of that must become firmly established in the heart, dominating and victorious, so that the heart not be forced to that (state). Rather, it should become like a lover from which the heart cannot be held back by force. Shibli said to his disciple, Husri: "If from Friday to Friday when you come to me you let anything pass in your heart other than God Most High, your